PRINCESS MARY

The Princess Royal, Countess of Harewood

Mary

Anna Robinson & Tara Hamilton Stubber

Contents

Princess Mary gardening on the Terrace at Harewood, 1960.

Foreword

FAMILY MEANT A LOT TO MY GRANDMOTHER. She was clearly fond of her grandsons – me, my brothers James and Jeremy, and our cousin Henry – but she was very undemonstrative in showing it, a result of her upbringing, not an expression of her true feelings.

We called her 'Ging Ging', a childish mangling of 'Grandma', and she did a pretty good job of tolerating our boisterousness as we bombed round the Terrace on our bicycles or made the chandeliers shake by playing football in the nursery at the top of the House. But when it came to mealtimes we had to behave ourselves. Table manners were very important and we were expected to know how to eat fish with two forks (no fish knives at Harewood!), and woe betide anyone who tore grapes off the bunch instead of snipping them with the special grape scissors.

She loved the countryside – a love she passed on – and would often take us for walks, into the woods or round the lake, spiking litter on the end of her walking stick and trying to persuade her dachshunds to walk to heel. On one such walk with my father and my two brothers in the spring of 1965, she suffered a fatal heart attack. I can't think of any better or more appropriate way to go. She was at heart a very private person, someone who couldn't stand 'fuss'; who you knew had to be treated with respect, but with a real sense of fun. Even as young boys we all could tell that under an exterior that could sometimes appear stern, there was real warmth and affection. I hope this publication gives some kind of insight into this very private person as well as the better known and much loved public servant.

DAVID LASCELLES, *Earl of Harewood*

☞ *Princess Mary and her grandsons (from the left) Henry, David, Jeremy and James with their dogs Astra, Wizzie and Debbie on the Terrace at Harewood. Standing to the left are Marion, first wife of Princess Mary's elder son, George (7th Earl of Harewood), and Angela, first wife of Princess Mary's younger son, Gerald, 1963. Photograph by Tom Blau, Camera Press London.*

The Royal Family on the balcony of Buckingham Palace celebrating the Silver Jubilee of King George V and Queen Mary, 6th May 1935.

Family Tree

VICTORIA *The Princess Royal* *The Empress Frederick* (1840-1901)	*m.* *1858*	FREDERICK *Emperor Frederick III* *of Germany & King of Prussia* (1831-1888)

ALBERT VICTOR
Duke of Clarence &
Avondale
(1864-1892)

EDWARD	ALBERT	*m.*	LADY ELIZABETH
KING EDWARD VIII	KING GEORGE VI	*1923*	BOWES-LYON
'David'	*'Bertie'*		QUEEN ELIZABETH
Abdicated January 1936	*Duke of York*		THE QUEEN MOTHER
Duke of Windsor	(1895-1952)		(1900-2002)
(1894-1972)			

HM QUEEN ELIZABETH II (b. 1926)	*m.* *1947*	HRH PRINCE PHILIP *of Greece and Denmark* DUKE OF EDINBURGH (b. 1921)	HRH PRINCESS MARGARET *Countess of Snowdon* (1930-2002)

CHARLES	ANNE	ANDREW	EDWARD
HRH The Prince of Wales	*HRH The Princess Royal*	*HRH The Duke of York*	*HRH The Earl of Wessex*
Heir Apparent	(b. 1950)	(b. 1960)	(b. 1964)
(b. 1948)			

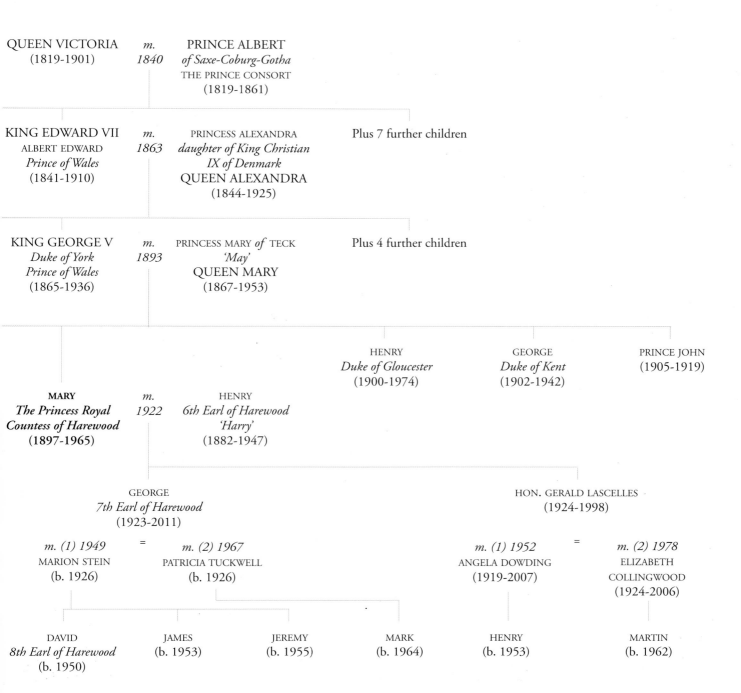

QUEEN VICTORIA
(1819-1901)

m.
1840

PRINCE ALBERT
of Saxe-Coburg-Gotha
THE PRINCE CONSORT
(1819-1861)

KING EDWARD VII
ALBERT EDWARD
Prince of Wales
(1841-1910)

m.
1863

PRINCESS ALEXANDRA
*daughter of King Christian
IX of Denmark*
QUEEN ALEXANDRA
(1844-1925)

Plus 7 further children

KING GEORGE V
*Duke of York
Prince of Wales*
(1865-1936)

m.
1893

PRINCESS MARY *of* TECK
'May'
QUEEN MARY
(1867-1953)

Plus 4 further children

HENRY
Duke of Gloucester
(1900-1974)

GEORGE
Duke of Kent
(1902-1942)

PRINCE JOHN
(1905-1919)

MARY
*The Princess Royal
Countess of Harewood*
(1897-1965)

m.
1922

HENRY
*6th Earl of Harewood
'Harry'*
(1882-1947)

GEORGE
7th Earl of Harewood
(1923-2011)

HON. GERALD LASCELLES
(1924-1998)

m. (1) 1949
MARION STEIN
(b. 1926)

=

m. (2) 1967
PATRICIA TUCKWELL
(b. 1926)

m. (1) 1952
ANGELA DOWDING
(1919-2007)

=

m. (2) 1978
ELIZABETH
COLLINGWOOD
(1924-2006)

DAVID
8th Earl of Harewood
(b. 1950)

JAMES
(b. 1953)

JEREMY
(b. 1955)

MARK
(b. 1964)

HENRY
(b. 1953)

MARTIN
(b. 1962)

Early Life

PRINCESS VICTORIA ALEXANDRA ALICE MARY OF YORK, was born at York Cottage on the Royal Estate of Sandringham on 25th April 1897. Princess Mary was the third of six children born to the Duke and Duchess of Kent (later King George V and Queen Mary), and their only daughter.

1897 was the year of Queen Victoria's Diamond Jubilee. The Queen called Princess Mary 'My little Diamond Jubilee Baby' and, as her great-grandmother and godmother, insisted that she be christened Victoria. It was only after Queen Victoria's death that the Princess became known as Mary, as her parents had wished.

ⓖ *Princess Mary with her mother Queen Mary and three younger brothers, 1905.*

ⓖⓖ *Queen Victoria and her great-grandchildren Prince Albert, Prince Edward and Princess Mary, 1897. Photograph by Robert Milne, © National Portrait Gallery, London.*

Princess Mary was brought up on the Sandringham Estate, where she and her five brothers enjoyed a relatively normal and active childhood. Her favourite outdoor pursuits included riding, cycling, ice skating and, when at Balmoral, fishing. She even asked her grandfather, King Edward VII, if she could learn to drive automobiles in Windsor Great Park, a request which he declined.

↻ Princess Mary and her brothers Prince Henry, Prince George and Prince John at Garden Cottage, Balmoral with members of the Royal Household staff Mr Watt (Tutor), 'Lalla' (Charlotte Bill, Nanny to Prince John), Miss Carse (Assistant Governess to Princess Mary), Mr Hansell (Tutor) and Mr Finch (Nursery Footman), 1910.

Princess Mary aboard HMY Alexandra, 1908.

Princess Mary and Prince John at Garden Cottage, Balmoral, 1910.

Princess Mary with her three younger brothers and her favourite childhood dog, Happy, in the gardens at Balmoral, 1910.

⟲ *Princess Mary learning to drive a dos-à-dos phaeton, Balmoral, 1909.*

⟰ *Princess Mary riding side-saddle on the beach with her brothers Prince Henry and Prince George, Sandringham, 1908.*

⟳ *Princess Mary Fishing at Balmoral, 1909.*

⟳⟳ *Princess Mary, Queen Mary and Sir Charles Frederick sampling apples, Sandringham, October 1911.*

⟳ *Prince Edward and Prince Henry ice skating, Sandringham, 1908.*

In 1910 King Edward VII died and Princess Mary's father was crowned King George V the following year. The family moved from Sandringham to Buckingham Palace, or 'Buckhouse Prison', as her brother David called it. Life became much more formal, with public ceremony and duty becoming part of everyday life for the young Princess.

GG *Princess Mary with her bicycle at Garden Cottage, Balmoral, 1910.*

G *Princess Mary, 1914. This is a portrait photograph of Princess Mary that was sent inside the gift boxes.*

Duty First

WARTIME SERVICE

IN 1914 BRITAIN DECLARED WAR AGAINST
GERMANY. King George V was adamant that
his family would do their utmost to support the war effort, even insisting that the Royal
Family should follow the same rationing regime as the rest of the nation.

Princess Mary was seventeen years old and keen to help in any way she could. She
decided to send a Christmas gift to every man and woman involved in the war effort on
Christmas Day 1914. Each gift consisted of a brass box containing a Christmas card and
either a pipe and tobacco, cigarettes or sweets. Princess Mary initially wanted to pay for
the boxes herself, but the project proved too large and a fund was established to which
she gave her name and support. In October 1914 Princess Mary made a public appeal
which raised £31,000 (approximately £3 million today) in just one week.

By the end of the war, 2.5 million gift boxes had been distributed, including some to
the families of those killed during active service. Some recipients chose to send their
gift boxes home to loved ones, while others kept theirs close by; one was even reported
to have saved a life when a bullet ricocheted off the brass box that the soldier was
carrying in his chest pocket. Today they are some of the most evocative mementos of
the First World War.

Princess Mary, Commandant-in-Chief of the British Red Cross, 1938.

Princess Mary's gift box and its contents, including tobacco, cigarettes, and monogrammed bullet pencil and writing case for non-smokers.

The card inside each box read: Wishing you a Happy Christmas and a Victorious New Year.

Princess Mary in the uniform of the Voluntary Aid Detachment, 1920. Princess Mary wore a red dress which signified her position as a commandant of the VAD.

NURSING

Princess Mary took particular interest in the Voluntary Aid Detachment (VAD). In 1917 a Voluntary Aid Detachment was formed at Buckingham Palace, comprised of thirty women personally recruited by Princess Mary, with her as Commandant.

In November 1918 Princess Mary travelled to France to visit hospitals and see the work of the VAD women in the field. Inspired by her war work, Princess Mary decided to train as a nurse at Great Ormond Street Hospital in London. Here she learnt every aspect of nursing care, and even trained to assist during surgery.

Princess Mary continued her nursing work as Patron of Great Ormond Street Hospital; Commandant-in-Chief of the British Red Cross Detachments, and in 1923 she lent her name to the nursing branch of the Royal Air Force, which became known as 'Princess Mary's Royal Air Force Nursing Service'.

Mary
1920.

MILITARY ROLES

From 1941 Princess Mary served with the British Army as Controller-Commandant of the Auxiliary Territorial Service (later the Women's Royal Army Corps) and held a number of honorary military positions, including Colonel-in-Chief of the Royal Scots and Colonel-in-Chief of the West Yorkshire Regiment. Princess Mary took a great personal interest in her troops and even wrote to the families of those who lost their lives in service. In 1949 the 10th Gurkha Rifles Regiment's name was changed to the 10th Princess Mary's Own Gurkha Rifles, as a mark of the outstanding contribution the regiment had made during the Second World War. Today this association continues with many retired Gurkhas and their families living and working at Harewood.

↻ Princess Mary enjoying tank training with the Royal Scots during the Second World War.
© Imperial War Museums (H 22720).

GIRL GUIDES

The Girl Guides Association was formed in 1910, and Princess Mary had a strong interest and involvement with it from an early age, becoming Norfolk's County Commissioner in 1917, aged twenty. After three years of devoted work she was made President of the organisation, a role she enjoyed throughout her life. In 1937, Princess Mary enrolled her nieces Princess Elizabeth as a Guide, and Princess Margaret as a Brownie, and the 1st Buckingham Palace Guide Company was formed.

A Royal Wedding

IN NOVEMBER 1921, THE ANNOUNCEMENT CAME FROM BUCKINGHAM PALACE that Princess Mary had become engaged to Henry, Viscount Lascelles, the elder son of the 5th Earl of Harewood.

Princess Mary's brother David (later Duke of Windsor) wrote to congratulate her on her good fortune:

"I'm so delighted to hear the marvellous news of your engagement… I must confess I am not surprised to hear it is Lascelles as he has so often been to Windsor and always asked to meet you… he is a splendid fellow.'

The Royal Wedding was set for 28th February 1922 and Princess Mary chose eight bridesmaids from her closest family and friends. Her cousins Lady Victoria Mary Cambridge, Lady May Cambridge and Princess Maud were chosen, as was Lady Mary Thynne, cousin of the groom. Her friends Lady Rachel Cavendish, Lady Doris Gordon-Lennox, Lady Diana Bridgeman and Lady Elizabeth Bowes-Lyon (Princess Mary's future sister-in-law) also joined the happy party.

⤴ *Princess Mary and Henry, Viscount Lascelles with the best man, Major Sir Victor Mackenzie, and Princess Mary's bridesmaids.*
From left: Lady Doris Gordon-Lennox, Lady May Cambridge, Lady Elizabeth Bowes-Lyon, Princess Maud, Lady Rachel Cavendish,
Lady Diana Bridgeman, Lady Mary Thynne, Lady Victoria Mary Cambridge, Buckingham Palace, 28th February 1922.

↶ *Princess Mary leaving Buckingham Palace with her father, King George V, for the wedding service at Westminster Abbey, 28th February 1922.*

↷ *Crowds outside Buckingham Palace and stretching down the Mall celebrating the Royal Wedding, 28th February 1922.*

↶ **The Mall**
Sir John Lavery
1922.

The Bridal Procession of Princess Mary and Viscount Lascelles. This painting was acquired by Viscount Lascelles after the wedding.

TO   150
WESTMINSTER ABBEY,
For those invited to be present at the Marriage of
HER ROYAL HIGHNESS THE PRINCESS MARY
with
THE VISCOUNT LASCELLES, D.S.O.

28th FEBRUARY, 1922.

THIS CARRIAGE,
to arrive before 10.45 a.m.
At the Dean's Yard Entrance to Westminster Abbey.

The Carriage to wait as the Police
may direct until called to take
up.

OVER

CARRIAGE TICKET.

The wedding took place at Westminster Abbey. The procession from Westminster Abbey to Buckingham Palace was a spectacular affair.

The streets were crowded, and after the deprivations of the First World War, people welcomed the chance to celebrate. As it was a February wedding, Princess Mary had few fresh flowers. During the procession she stopped the carriage and asked for her bouquet of pink sweet peas to be placed at the Cenotaph, a mark of respect to those who had died during the First World War.

Princess Mary wrote to her former tutor Mr Hansell:
'I cannot tell you how happy I am and I feel that I am very lucky. I feel sure that you will like my Harry.'

⬆ *The official wedding photograph: Princess Mary and Viscount Lascelles with King George V and Queen Mary in the Throne Room at Buckingham Palace, 28th February 1922.*

⮕ *Princess Mary and Viscount Lascelles departing for their honeymoon in Italy.*

PRINCESS MARY'S WEDDING DRESS

Princess Mary's wedding dress was made by the English fashion house Reville of London; the designer was William Wallace Terry, Court Dressmaker to Queen Mary.

The dress was described by Vogue as a combination of *youthful simplicity and Royal Splendour.* It consisted of a silver lamé underdress decorated with silver thread and beads on its lower edge and an ivory silk marquisette overdress embellished with a rose trellis design in crystal beads and pearls.

The long silk train was woven at Braintree silk mills using white and silver threads to create a pattern of flowers emblematic of the British Empire, including the English rose, the Welsh daffodil, the Canadian maple and the New Zealand fern. The woven silk was enhanced by Indian lotuses embroidered in silver thread. Finally, the train was edged with Honiton lace, a gift from Queen Mary that was later removed for another royal bride to use.

❦❦ *Princess Mary's tiara. The simple frame is wrapped with silver wire and then decorated with wax and silk orange blossom flowers and buds.*

❦❦ *The dress was designed to hang from the shoulders, and had a twisted silver and pearl beaded belt, with silk orange blossom flowers attached to one side. Orange blossom is traditionally used at weddings as a symbol of good fortune.*

Life in Yorkshire

AFTER THEIR HONEYMOON IN ITALY Viscount Lascelles (known as Harry) and Princess Mary moved to Goldsborough Hall, a Lascelles family home in Yorkshire. In 1923 their first son, George, was born, and a second son, Gerald, followed a year later in 1924.

George, 7th Earl of Harewood recalled a happy childhood at Goldsborough:

'My earliest childhood memories are bound up with Goldsborough: smells, which I have since realised are the most evocative of all associations… the peacocks which roamed the gardens until my father connected a barren year's racing with them and superstitiously decided on their removal; the Guernsey cows from which came our too-rich milk and which roamed the park and terrorised our nanny; the elegant but slightly ludicrous Irish wolfhounds which my mother had been given.'

He also eloquently described his mother:

'Shyness, I should imagine, was one of the first things people noticed about my mother; gentleness and kindness as well, with in later life a little Hanoverian spleen underneath it all… That my mother's interest in Family was inculcated early on I have no doubt, as with Queen Mary it was very strong indeed.'

Princess Mary and Harry with their sons George and new-born Gerald, 1924.

HAREWOOD

In 1929, upon the death of the 5th Earl of Harewood, Harry inherited the Harewood Estate and in 1930 he and Princess Mary moved to Harewood. As the 6th Earl and Countess of Harewood they began a programme of modernisation and improvement throughout the House and Estate.

In the House, bathrooms were installed, the kitchens modernised and new heating systems replaced outdated ones. In the East Wing of the House, a new suite of rooms was designed for Princess Mary by the eminent architect Herbert Baker. She worked closely with Baker on every detail of the design: the addition of coats of arms in the apse, her monogram and emblems of the United Kingdom and Commonwealth countries on the ceilings, even the inclusion of the motifs of the Royal Scots and the Girl Guides in her bathroom.

↺ *George and Gerald in the gardens at Goldsborough, c.1927.*

↻ *Princess Mary, Harry, George and Gerald at Goldsborough, c.1930.*

↺ *Princess Mary driving George and Gerald in her pony trap, Goldsborough, c.1928.*
© *Associated Newspapers/ Solo Syndication.*

↻ *Princess Mary, George and Gerald at Harewood, c.1934.*

⟳ Princess Mary and Harry on the Terrace at Harewood, 1946

⟳ Princess Mary and cowman Harry Todd inspecting a Red Poll heifer, c.1960.

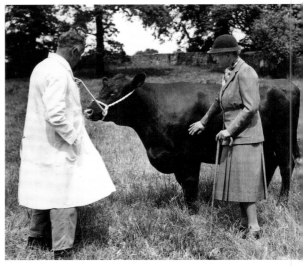

28

In the Grounds, work began on building new glasshouses in the Walled Garden, planting the Terrace with roses, and creating the Rock Garden at the head of the Lake (now the Himalayan Garden). During Princess Mary and Harry's tenure, the estate became increasingly productive and the Home Farm became home to Princess Mary's prize herd of Red Poll cattle.

↻ Harewood Estate Tenants and Staff, September 1930. Princess Mary and Harry are seated in the middle front row with their elder son, George, between them.

Her son George wrote:

'Most mornings from the time I was twelve until after the beginning of the war my mother used to come riding with us. She rode with skill, and we had a certain sense of pride when we were considered old and responsible enough to go out with her alone and without a groom – an odd source of satisfaction that sounds now!'

'Gardening was one of the things my parents liked to do together and when Gerald and I were children we used to go out with them in the afternoon and help reduce unruly thickets of rhododendrons to manageable proportions… When she grew older, it was the pruning of the roses my mother preferred to the removal of over-exuberant rhododendrons, and she would go off pruning on a summer evening with a lady-in-waiting while we played tennis.'

↻ **Princess Mary on Portumna**
Sir Alfred Munnings
1930.

➔ *Princess Mary on her last foreign tour at Victoria Falls, Zambia 1964. Princess Mary represented HM The Queen at the Independence Ceremony of Zambia.*

ROYAL DUTIES

Princess Mary's strong commitment to public duty meant her life was always busy. As a wife, a mother and daughter of the King, she divided her time between Yorkshire, London, and her duties overseas.

In 1932 Princess Mary received the title Princess Royal from her father King George V. It was a mark of her position as the daughter of the monarch and an active member of the Royal Family. During her lifetime she would know six monarchs: her great-grandmother Queen Victoria, her grandfather King Edward VII, her father King George V, her brothers King Edward VIII and later King George VI, and her niece HM Queen Elizabeth II.

↻ *The Princess Royal was an important figure at royal events, including the Coronation of King George VI in 1937, when her sons attended the King as pages. Here she attended as both a peeress and sister of the King.*

↻↻ *Visiting the Cairo Museum with M. Lacau, Director of Antiquities, during a tour of Egypt, April 1928.*

A Passion for Collecting

PRINCESS MARY'S MOTHER QUEEN MARY WAS AN ENTHUSIASTIC COLLECTOR and her love of beautiful objects was something she passed on to her daughter. Princess Mary began collecting from an early age and during her life acquired an array of beautiful pieces including jade, fans, Fabergé and watercolours.

Princess Mary adored owls and collected a great number throughout her life. Her collection adorned her private rooms and owls were often given to Princess Mary as personal gifts by family and friends.

⊃ *Princess Mary's Sitting Room at Harewood House (now the State Bedroom). This room was converted in the 1840s into the Countess's Sitting Room. Princess Mary was the last Countess of Harewood to use the room as her personal study.*

⊅ *Princess Mary's Fabergé owls. From the left: a quartz owl with ruby eyes wearing an enamelled night cap and set on a nephrite base; a carved banded agate owl with ruby eyes; a carved agate owl with emerald eyes.*

The City of Leeds emblem was also that of an owl, a happy coincidence for a princess who once said of Yorkshire: *'If I could choose anywhere in the world to live it would be here, the best place.'*

FABERGÉ

Peter Carl Fabergé was goldsmith and jeweller to the Russia Imperial Court from 1885 until the Russian Revolution in 1917. He died shortly afterwards in exile in Switzerland. The exquisite artefacts of gold, enamel and individually set precious stones that he created were admired and adored across Europe. The British Royal Family were among his most important patrons. King George V and Queen Mary were avid collectors, often exchanging gifts of Fabergé at times of celebration.

A pair of banded agate owls with ruby eyes, mounted on a gold branch and quartz base by Fabergé, with workmaster's mark of Henrik Wigström, c.1908.

Queen Mary purchased this pair of owls from the Fabergé emporium in 1908 as a gift. The piece was later sold and acquired by Harry for Princess Mary in 1946.

↰↱ *A miniature gold and guilloche enamel expanding photograph frame pendant by Fabergé containing photographs of the Duke of Gloucester, the Duke of York, King George V, the Prince of Wales, Princess Mary and the Duke of Kent.*

The pendant was acquired on 21st November 1912 for the sum of £23 from the London branch of Fabergé. It was possibly given to King George V's mother, Queen Alexandra, for her birthday on 1st December and these photographs inserted later.

FANS

Princess Mary's wedding gifts included forty-one feather, lace and antique silk fans. The act of giving a fan was part of a long tradition of commemorating religious, ceremonial or royal occasions and, in particular, the marriage of a royal bride.

↺ *This white ostrich fan was often held by Princess Mary in formal portraits of the 1920s. It was a wedding gift from the Ostrich Farmers of South Africa.*

↪ *Princess Mary, 1922.*

Many of the painted fans given to Princess Mary date from the 18th and 19th centuries. By the early 20th century painted fans were out of fashion, though many people still appreciated their beauty, not least Queen Mary, whose collection was one of the finest in the country.

During the 1920s and 1930s, Princess Mary was often seen on public occasions carrying extravagant ostrich-feather fans made by Duvelleroy and Cartier. Made specially for her, they were often adorned with her monogram or name set in precious stones.

Ivory and silk painted fan, c.1780. This French fan was a wedding gift. It is painted with small vignettes and embellished with sequins, embroidered with straw and mounted on gilded carved ivory sticks.

PAINTINGS

In 1916, upon the death of his great-uncle the 2nd Marquess of Clanricarde, Henry, Viscount Lascelles unexpectedly inherited a large fortune. It was with this bequest that he began collecting Italian paintings, works which were to form one of the greatest 20th century collections of Renaissance paintings in England.

Princess Mary and Harry shared a love of art, and throughout their marriage collected Old Masters and English watercolours. During the 1920s and 1930s they bought back many of the watercolours of Harewood painted by JMW Turner and Thomas Girtin between 1797 and *c.*1806, which had been sold during the Victorian period.

The Reconciliation of the Romans and Sabine with the marriage of Romulus and Hersilia The Master of Marradi *c.*1460.

One of a pair of Florentine Cassone (marriage chest) panels purchased by Viscount Lascelles and Princess Mary in 1923.

⟳ **Harewood House
from the South West**
J.M.W. Turner
1798.

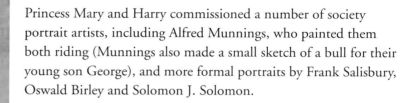

Princess Mary and Harry commissioned a number of society portrait artists, including Alfred Munnings, who painted them both riding (Munnings also made a small sketch of a bull for their young son George), and more formal portraits by Frank Salisbury, Oswald Birley and Solomon J. Solomon.

The collections of the 6th Earl and Princess Mary are an important part of Harewood's story of patronage of the arts, a family tradition that continues to the present day

G **HRH The Princess Royal on 'Portumna' and the Earl of Harewood, Master of Bramham Moor Hunt on 'Tommy'**
Sir Alfred Munnings
© Estate of Sir Alfred Munnings. All rights reserved, DACS 2014.

Commissioned by Princess Mary and 6th Earl c.1931.

Later Years

IN 1939 WAR BROKE OUT WITH GERMANY AND LIFE AT HAREWOOD CHANGED FOR EVER. Harewood became a convalescent hospital, as it had been during the First World War, and Princess Mary and Harry refocused the Estate's resources to help the war effort.

Harewood remained a hospital until 1947, the same year Princess Mary and Harry celebrated their silver wedding anniversary in Torquay. Shortly afterwards, Harry contracted pneumonia and died, leaving Princess Mary a widow at the age of fifty.

↻ Visitors queuing to see the State Rooms, Harewood House, 1951.

At that time, death duties of seventy per cent were payable on all inherited wealth, and Harry's death meant that large parts of the Harewood Estate and some of the contents of Harewood House had to be sold to pay the tax owed.

Princess Mary continued to live at Harewood with her son George, 7th Earl of Harewood and his new family. Four grandsons were born during the 1950s. Harewood House opened to the public, the first royal residence to do so, and visitors flocked to see the home of the Princess Royal. Royal duties continued, but Princess Mary spent as much time as she could with her family; gardening, walking her dogs and enjoying the Yorkshire countryside.

One day in the spring of 1965, as she was walking round the Lake with her son and two grandsons, Princess Mary suffered a fatal heart attack.

Not long before she died she wrote:

My love for this part of Yorkshire has become such an integral part of my life that it would be a great sorrow for me to contemplate making my home elsewhere.

The affection was reciprocated by the people of Yorkshire and she is still known as 'The Yorkshire Princess'.

↪ *Princess Mary and her son George, 7th Earl of Harewood, on the Terrace at Harewood, 1949.*

**6th Earl of Harewood
and Princess Mary**
John Singer Sargent
1923-1925.

44